This Dance Journal Belongs To

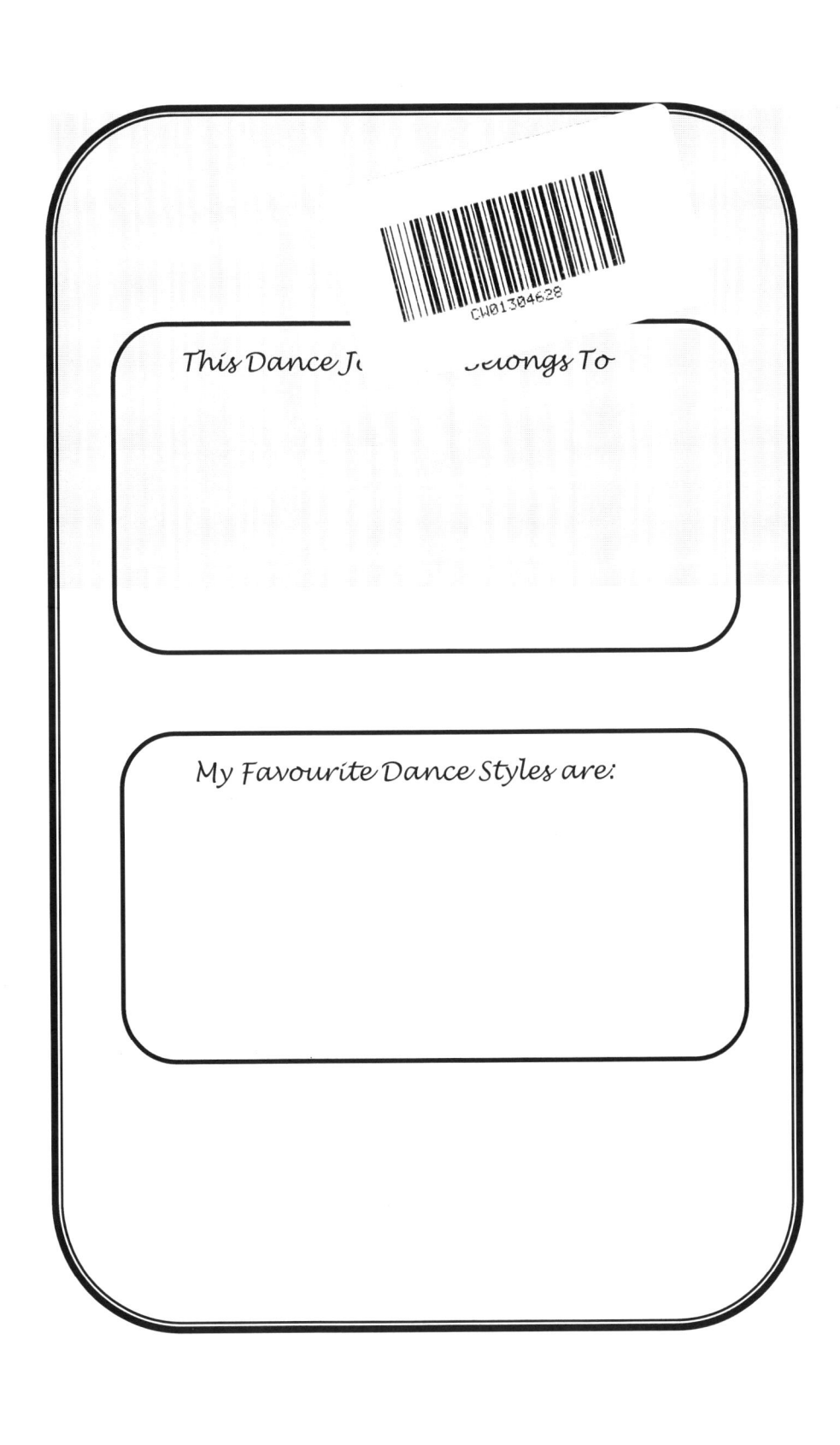

My Favourite Dance Styles are:

Lesson Date   *Teacher Name*

Technical Notes:

Corrections given - New Terminology – Goals before next Class

Artistic Notes:

Coaching (personal or ensemble) - choreographic notes

Reflections and Goals:

Thoughts - Progress made against dance goals - Inspiration

Next Class:

Questions – Terminology not Understood – What to work On

FAQ

Lesson Date *Teacher Name*

― ― ― ― ― ―   ― ― ― ― ―

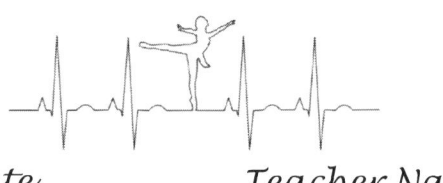

Technical Notes:

Corrections given - New Terminology – Goals before next Class

Artistic Notes:

Coaching (personal or ensemble) - choreographic notes

Reflections and Goals:

Thoughts - Progress made against dance goals - Inspiration

Next Class:

Questions – Terminology not Understood – What to work On

FAQ

Lesson Date   *Teacher Name*

Technical Notes:

Corrections given - New Terminology – Goals before next Class

Artistic Notes:

Coaching (personal or ensemble) - choreographic notes

Reflections and Goals:

Thoughts - Progress made against dance goals - Inspiration

Next Class:

Questions – Terminology not Understood – What to work On

FAQ

Lesson Date   *Teacher Name*

–––––   –––––

Technical Notes:

Corrections given - New Terminology – Goals before next Class

Artistic Notes:

Coaching (personal or ensemble) - choreographic notes

Reflections and Goals:

Thoughts - Progress made against dance goals - Inspiration

Next Class:

Questions – Terminology not Understood – What to work On

FAQ

Lesson Date — Teacher Name

Technical Notes:

Corrections given - New Terminology – Goals before next Class

Artistic Notes:

Coaching (personal or ensemble) - choreographic notes

Reflections and Goals:

Thoughts - Progress made against dance goals - Inspiration

Next Class:

Questions – Terminology not Understood – What to work On

FAQ

Lesson Date   *Teacher Name*

Technical Notes:

Corrections given - New Terminology – Goals before next Class

Artistic Notes:

Coaching (personal or ensemble) - choreographic notes

Reflections and Goals:

Thoughts - Progress made against dance goals - Inspiration

Next Class:

Questions – Terminology not Understood – What to work On

FAQ

Lesson Date   *Teacher Name*

------------   ------------

Technical Notes:

Corrections given - New Terminology – Goals before next Class

Artistic Notes:

Coaching (personal or ensemble) - choreographic notes

Reflections and Goals:

Thoughts - Progress made against dance goals - Inspiration

Next Class:

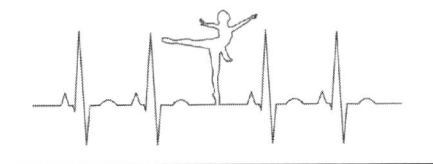

Questions – Terminology not Understood – What to work On

FAQ

Lesson Date   *Teacher Name*

_ _ _ _ _ _   _ _ _ _ _ _

Technical Notes:

Corrections given - New Terminology – Goals before next Class

Artistic Notes:

Coaching (personal or ensemble) - choreographic notes

Reflections and Goals:

Thoughts - Progress made against dance goals - Inspiration

Next Class:

Questions – Terminology not Understood – What to work On

FAQ

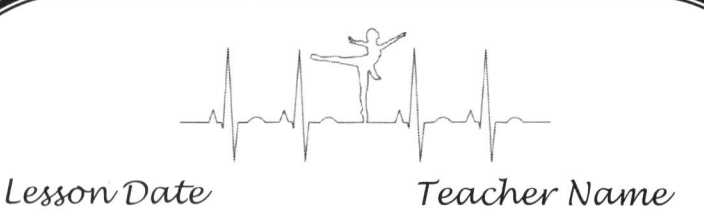

Lesson Date   *Teacher Name*

――――――― ―――――――

Technical Notes:

Corrections given - New Terminology – Goals before next Class

Artistic Notes:

Coaching (personal or ensemble) - choreographic notes

Reflections and Goals:

Thoughts - Progress made against dance goals - Inspiration

Next Class:

Questions – Terminology not Understood – What to work On

FAQ

Lesson Date   *Teacher Name*

― ― ― ― ―   ― ― ― ―

Technical Notes:

Corrections given - New Terminology – Goals before next Class

Artistic Notes:

Coaching (personal or ensemble) - choreographic notes

Reflections and Goals:

Thoughts - Progress made against dance goals - Inspiration

Next Class:

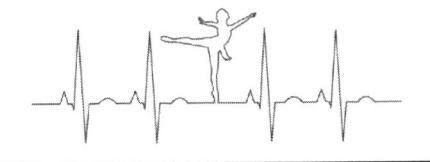

Questions – Terminology not Understood – What to work On

FAQ

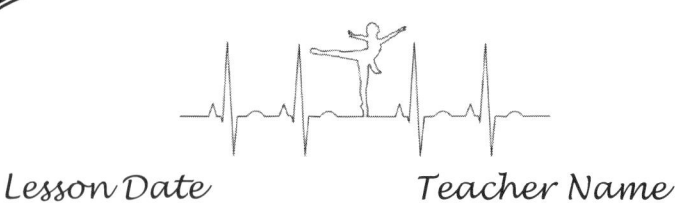

Lesson Date   *Teacher Name*

Technical Notes:

Corrections given - New Terminology – Goals before next Class

Artistic Notes:

Coaching (personal or ensemble) - choreographic notes

Reflections and Goals:

Thoughts - Progress made against dance goals - Inspiration

Next Class:

Questions – Terminology not Understood – What to work On

FAQ

Lesson Date   *Teacher Name*

Technical Notes:

Corrections given - New Terminology – Goals before next Class

Artistic Notes:

Coaching (personal or ensemble) - choreographic notes

Reflections and Goals:

Thoughts - Progress made against dance goals - Inspiration

Next Class:

Questions – Terminology not Understood – What to work On

FAQ

Lesson Date   Teacher Name

_ _ _ _ _ _   _ _ _ _ _ _

Technical Notes:

Corrections given - New Terminology – Goals before next Class

Artistic Notes:

Coaching (personal or ensemble) - choreographic notes

Reflections and Goals:

Thoughts - Progress made against dance goals - Inspiration

Next Class:

Questions – Terminology not Understood – What to work On

FAQ

Lesson Date *Teacher Name*

–––––– ––––––

Technical Notes:

Corrections given - New Terminology – Goals before next Class

Artistic Notes:

Coaching (personal or ensemble) - choreographic notes

Reflections and Goals:

Thoughts - Progress made against dance goals - Inspiration

Next Class:

Questions – Terminology not Understood – What to work On

FAQ

Lesson Date   *Teacher Name*

---------   ---------

Technical Notes:

Corrections given - New Terminology - Goals before next Class

Artistic Notes:

Coaching (personal or ensemble) - choreographic notes

Reflections and Goals:

Thoughts - Progress made against dance goals - Inspiration

Next Class:

Questions – Terminology not Understood – What to work On

FAQ

Lesson Date   *Teacher Name*

–––––––––– ––––––––––

Technical Notes:

Corrections given - New Terminology – Goals before next Class

Artistic Notes:

Coaching (personal or ensemble) - choreographic notes

Reflections and Goals:

Thoughts - Progress made against dance goals - Inspiration

Next Class:

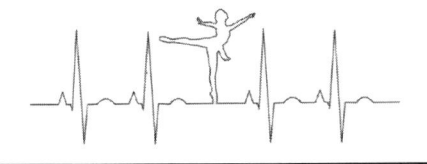

Questions – Terminology not Understood – What to work On

FAQ

Lesson Date   *Teacher Name*

Technical Notes:

Corrections given - New Terminology – Goals before next Class

Artistic Notes:

Coaching (personal or ensemble) - choreographic notes

Reflections and Goals:

Thoughts - Progress made against dance goals - Inspiration

Next Class:

Questions – Terminology not Understood – What to work On

FAQ

Lesson Date   *Teacher Name*

_____ _____

Technical Notes:

Corrections given - New Terminology – Goals before next Class

Artistic Notes:

Coaching (personal or ensemble) - choreographic notes

Reflections and Goals:

Thoughts - Progress made against dance goals - Inspiration

Next Class:

Questions – Terminology not Understood – What to work On

FAQ

Lesson Date   Teacher Name

_ _ _ _ _ _ _ _   _ _ _ _ _ _

Technical Notes:

Corrections given - New Terminology – Goals before next Class

Artistic Notes:

Coaching (personal or ensemble) - choreographic notes

Reflections and Goals:

Thoughts - Progress made against dance goals - Inspiration

Next Class:

Questions – Terminology not Understood – What to work On

FAQ

Lesson Date   *Teacher Name*

― ― ― ― ―   ― ― ― ― ―

Technical Notes:

Corrections given - New Terminology – Goals before next Class

Artistic Notes:

Coaching (personal or ensemble) - choreographic notes

Reflections and Goals:

Thoughts - Progress made against dance goals - Inspiration

Next Class:

Questions – Terminology not Understood – What to work On

FAQ

Lesson Date   *Teacher Name*

―――――   ―――――

Technical Notes:

Corrections given - New Terminology – Goals before next Class

Artistic Notes:

Coaching (personal or ensemble) - choreographic notes

Reflections and Goals:

Thoughts - Progress made against dance goals - Inspiration

Next Class:

Questions – Terminology not Understood – What to work On

FAQ

Lesson Date *Teacher Name*

_ _ _ _ _ _ _ _   _ _ _ _ _ _

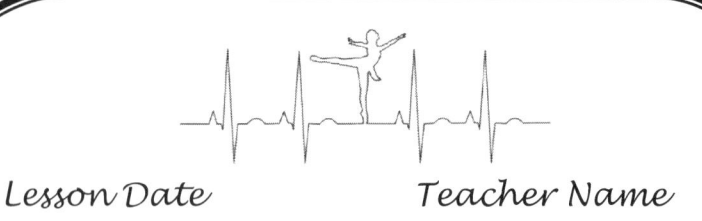

Technical Notes:

Corrections given - New Terminology – Goals before next Class

Artistic Notes:

Coaching (personal or ensemble) - choreographic notes

Reflections and Goals:

Thoughts - Progress made against dance goals - Inspiration

Next Class:

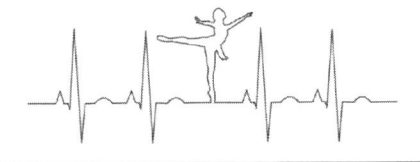

Questions – Terminology not Understood – What to work On

FAQ

Lesson Date   *Teacher Name*

_____   _____

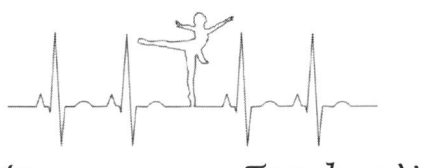

Technical Notes:

Corrections given - New Terminology – Goals before next Class

Artistic Notes:

Coaching (personal or ensemble) - choreographic notes

Reflections and Goals:

Thoughts - Progress made against dance goals - Inspiration

Next Class:

Questions – Terminology not Understood – What to work On

FAQ

Lesson Date   *Teacher Name*

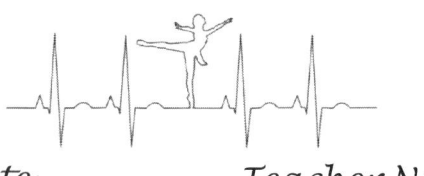

_____   _____

Technical Notes:

Corrections given - New Terminology – Goals before next Class

Artistic Notes:

Coaching (personal or ensemble) - choreographic notes

Reflections and Goals:

Thoughts - Progress made against dance goals - Inspiration

Next Class:

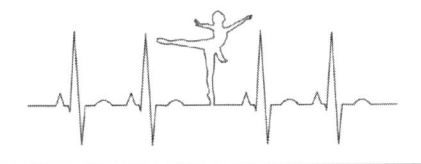

Questions – Terminology not Understood – What to work On

FAQ

Lesson Date   *Teacher Name*

― ― ― ― ―   ― ― ― ― ―

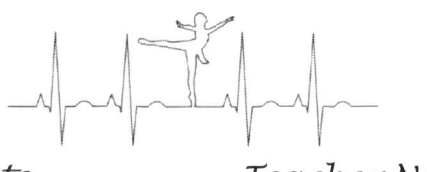

Technical Notes:

Corrections given - New Terminology – Goals before next Class

Artistic Notes:

Coaching (personal or ensemble) - choreographic notes

Reflections and Goals:

Thoughts - Progress made against dance goals - Inspiration

Next Class:

Questions – Terminology not Understood – What to work On

FAQ

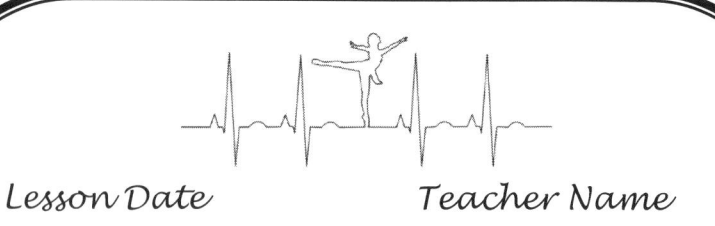

Lesson Date   *Teacher Name*

----------   ----------

Technical Notes:

Corrections given - New Terminology – Goals before next Class

Artistic Notes:

Coaching (personal or ensemble) - choreographic notes

Reflections and Goals:

Thoughts - Progress made against dance goals - Inspiration

Next Class:

Questions – Terminology not Understood – What to work On

FAQ

Lesson Date _ _ _ _ _ _   Teacher Name _ _ _ _ _ _

Technical Notes:

Corrections given - New Terminology – Goals before next Class

Artistic Notes:

Coaching (personal or ensemble) - choreographic notes

Reflections and Goals:

Thoughts - Progress made against dance goals - Inspiration

Next Class:

Questions – Terminology not Understood – What to work On

FAQ

Lesson Date   *Teacher Name*

_____   _____

Technical Notes:

Corrections given - New Terminology – Goals before next Class

Artistic Notes:

Coaching (personal or ensemble) - choreographic notes

Reflections and Goals:

Thoughts - Progress made against dance goals - Inspiration

Next Class:

Questions – Terminology not Understood – What to work On

FAQ

Lesson Date *Teacher Name*

――― ―――

Technical Notes:

Corrections given - New Terminology – Goals before next Class

Artistic Notes:

Coaching (personal or ensemble) - choreographic notes

Reflections and Goals:

Thoughts - Progress made against dance goals - Inspiration

Next Class:

Questions – Terminology not Understood – What to work On

FAQ

Lesson Date   *Teacher Name*

_____   _____

Technical Notes:

Corrections given - New Terminology – Goals before next Class

Artistic Notes:

Coaching (personal or ensemble) - choreographic notes

Reflections and Goals:

Thoughts - Progress made against dance goals - Inspiration

Next Class:

Questions – Terminology not Understood – What to work On

FAQ

Lesson Date   *Teacher Name*

-------   -------

Technical Notes:

Corrections given - New Terminology – Goals before next Class

Artistic Notes:

Coaching (personal or ensemble) - choreographic notes

Reflections and Goals:

Thoughts - Progress made against dance goals - Inspiration

Next Class:

Questions – Terminology not Understood – What to work On

FAQ

Lesson Date   *Teacher Name*

_____   _____

Technical Notes:

Corrections given - New Terminology - Goals before next Class

Artistic Notes:

Coaching (personal or ensemble) - choreographic notes

Reflections and Goals:

Thoughts - Progress made against dance goals - Inspiration

Next Class:

Questions – Terminology not Understood – What to work On

FAQ

Lesson Date   *Teacher Name*

_ _ _ _ _ _   _ _ _ _ _ _

Technical Notes:

Corrections given - New Terminology - Goals before next Class

Artistic Notes:

Coaching (personal or ensemble) - choreographic notes

Reflections and Goals:

Thoughts - Progress made against dance goals - Inspiration

Next Class:

Questions – Terminology not Understood – What to work On

FAQ

Lesson Date   *Teacher Name*

__ __ __ __ __   __ __ __ __ __

Technical Notes:

Corrections given - New Terminology – Goals before next Class

Artistic Notes:

Coaching (personal or ensemble) - choreographic notes

Reflections and Goals:

Thoughts - Progress made against dance goals - Inspiration

Next Class:

Questions – Terminology not Understood – What to work On

FAQ

Lesson Date   *Teacher Name*

_____   _____

Technical Notes:

Corrections given - New Terminology - Goals before next Class

Artistic Notes:

Coaching (personal or ensemble) - choreographic notes

Reflections and Goals:

Thoughts - Progress made against dance goals - Inspiration

Next Class:

Questions – Terminology not Understood – What to work On

FAQ

Lesson Date   *Teacher Name*

_____   _____

Technical Notes:

Corrections given - New Terminology – Goals before next Class

Artistic Notes:

Coaching (personal or ensemble) - choreographic notes

Reflections and Goals:

Thoughts - Progress made against dance goals - Inspiration

Next Class:

Questions – Terminology not Understood – What to work On

FAQ

Lesson Date   *Teacher Name*

_____   _____

Technical Notes:

Corrections given - New Terminology – Goals before next Class

Artistic Notes:

Coaching (personal or ensemble) - choreographic notes

Reflections and Goals:

Thoughts - Progress made against dance goals - Inspiration

Next Class:

Questions – Terminology not Understood – What to work On

FAQ

Lesson Date   *Teacher Name*

-------   -------

Technical Notes:

Corrections given - New Terminology – Goals before next Class

Artistic Notes:

Coaching (personal or ensemble) - choreographic notes

Reflections and Goals:

Thoughts - Progress made against dance goals - Inspiration

Next Class:

Questions – Terminology not Understood – What to work On

FAQ

Lesson Date   *Teacher Name*

―――――   ―――――

Technical Notes:

Corrections given - New Terminology – Goals before next Class

Artistic Notes:

Coaching (personal or ensemble) - choreographic notes

Reflections and Goals:

Thoughts - Progress made against dance goals - Inspiration

Next Class:

Questions – Terminology not Understood – What to work On

FAQ

Lesson Date   *Teacher Name*

_ _ _ _ _ _   _ _ _ _ _ _

Technical Notes:

Corrections given - New Terminology – Goals before next Class

Artistic Notes:

Coaching (personal or ensemble) - choreographic notes

Reflections and Goals:

Thoughts - Progress made against dance goals - Inspiration

Next Class:

Questions – Terminology not Understood – What to work On

FAQ

Lesson Date   *Teacher Name*

―――――   ―――――

Technical Notes:

Corrections given - New Terminology – Goals before next Class

Artistic Notes:

Coaching (personal or ensemble) - choreographic notes

Reflections and Goals:

Thoughts - Progress made against dance goals - Inspiration

Next Class:

Questions – Terminology not Understood – What to work On

FAQ

Lesson Date   *Teacher Name*

―――――   ―――――

Technical Notes:

Corrections given - New Terminology – Goals before next Class

Artistic Notes:

Coaching (personal or ensemble) - choreographic notes

Reflections and Goals:

Thoughts - Progress made against dance goals - Inspiration

Next Class:

Questions – Terminology not Understood – What to work On

FAQ

Lesson Date   *Teacher Name*

-----------   -----------

Technical Notes:

Corrections given - New Terminology – Goals before next Class

Artistic Notes:

Coaching (personal or ensemble) - choreographic notes

Reflections and Goals:

Thoughts - Progress made against dance goals - Inspiration

Next Class:

Questions – Terminology not Understood – What to work On

FAQ

Lesson Date   *Teacher Name*

——————— ———————

Technical Notes:

Corrections given - New Terminology – Goals before next Class

Artistic Notes:

Coaching (personal or ensemble) - choreographic notes

Reflections and Goals:

Thoughts - Progress made against dance goals - Inspiration

Next Class:

Questions – Terminology not Understood – What to work On

FAQ

Lesson Date   *Teacher Name*

——————— ———————

Technical Notes:

Corrections given - New Terminology – Goals before next Class

Artistic Notes:

Coaching (personal or ensemble) - choreographic notes

Reflections and Goals:

Thoughts - Progress made against dance goals - Inspiration

Next Class:

Questions – Terminology not Understood – What to work On

FAQ

Lesson Date *Teacher Name*

Technical Notes:

Corrections given - New Terminology – Goals before next Class

Artistic Notes:

Coaching (personal or ensemble) - choreographic notes

Reflections and Goals:

Thoughts - Progress made against dance goals - Inspiration

Next Class:

Questions – Terminology not Understood – What to work On

FAQ

Lesson Date   *Teacher Name*

-------   -------

Technical Notes:

Corrections given - New Terminology – Goals before next Class

Artistic Notes:

Coaching (personal or ensemble) - choreographic notes

Reflections and Goals:

Thoughts - Progress made against dance goals - Inspiration

Next Class:

Questions – Terminology not Understood – What to work On

FAQ

Lesson Date   *Teacher Name*

-----------   -----------

Technical Notes:

Corrections given - New Terminology – Goals before next Class

Artistic Notes:

Coaching (personal or ensemble) - choreographic notes

Reflections and Goals:

Thoughts - Progress made against dance goals - Inspiration

Next Class:

Questions – Terminology not Understood – What to work On

FAQ

Lesson Date   *Teacher Name*

_____   _____

Technical Notes:

Corrections given - New Terminology – Goals before next Class

Artistic Notes:

Coaching (personal or ensemble) - choreographic notes

Reflections and Goals:

Thoughts - Progress made against dance goals - Inspiration

Next Class:

Questions – Terminology not Understood – What to work On

FAQ

Lesson Date   *Teacher Name*

_____   _____

Technical Notes:

Corrections given - New Terminology – Goals before next Class

Artistic Notes:

Coaching (personal or ensemble) - choreographic notes

Reflections and Goals:

Thoughts - Progress made against dance goals - Inspiration

Next Class:

Questions – Terminology not Understood – What to work On

FAQ

Lesson Date   *Teacher Name*

_ _ _ _ _ _ _   _ _ _ _ _ _

Technical Notes:

Corrections given - New Terminology – Goals before next Class

Artistic Notes:

Coaching (personal or ensemble) - choreographic notes

Reflections and Goals:

Thoughts - Progress made against dance goals - Inspiration

Next Class:

Questions – Terminology not Understood – What to work On

FAQ

Lesson Date   *Teacher Name*

_____   _____

Technical Notes:

Corrections given - New Terminology – Goals before next Class

Artistic Notes:

Coaching (personal or ensemble) - choreographic notes

Reflections and Goals:

Thoughts - Progress made against dance goals - Inspiration

Next Class:

Questions – Terminology not Understood – What to work On

FAQ

Space for Your Lists

List Ideas:
- Helpful stretches and strengthening ideas
- Research (dancers, companies, videos, songs)
- Funny and inspirational quotes
- Wishlist
- Competition Prep

Space for Your Lists

Printed in Great Britain
by Amazon